PACKING A SUITCASE FOR THE AFTERLIFE

poems by

Colleen Redman

Finishing Line Press
Georgetown, Kentucky

PACKING A SUITCASE FOR THE AFTERLIFE

Copyright © 2017 by Colleen Redman
ISBN 978-1-63534-287-1 First Edition
All rights reserved under International and Pan-American Copyright Conventions.
No part of this book may be reproduced in any manner whatsoever without written permission from the publisher, except in the case of brief quotations embodied in critical articles and reviews.

ACKNOWLEDGMENTS

Ghost Poem first appeared in the 2016 issue of *Artemis Journal*.
Waiting to Be Saved previously appeared in the *Floyd County Moonshine*.
Never Too Late previously appeared in 2017 issue *757 Perspectives, Volume II: Evolutions*.
Where I'm From was inspired by George Ella Lyon's poem of the same name in the book *Where I'm From, Where Poems Come From*.
The Girl Next Door appeared on *The Front Porch Review* in April 2016.
The Collector appeared in the 2014 issue of *Artemis Journal* and was chosen for Poems for the Waiting Room, a U.K. Arts in Health charity that provides poems for patients.
Second Hand Chance appeared on *Poets Haven* in December 2016.
I Put You on Speaker Phone first appeared in *Floyd County Moonshine* literary magazine.
Be Hold was previously published in the July 2016 issue of *The Front Porch Review*.

Publisher: Leah Maines
Editor: Christen Kincaid
Cover Art: Joe Klein
Author Photo: Colleen Redman
Cover Design: Elizabeth Maines McCleavy

Printed in the USA on acid-free paper.
Order online: www.finishinglinepress.com
also available on amazon.com

Author inquiries and mail orders:
Finishing Line Press
P. O. Box 1626
Georgetown, Kentucky 40324
U. S. A.

Table of Contents

Ghost Poem 1
Black Bear 2
Teacher's Pet 3
Flying Dreams 4
Monsters Under the Bed 5
I Don't See Blue 6
I Look Up 7
How to Make a Freckle 8
Waiting to Be Saved 9
I'm Drawing on the Blank Slate of This Day 10
Never Too Late 11
Going Home 12
The Suitcase 13
Morning Commute 14
Dream Inventory 15
Where I'm From 16
Jim and Dan 18
The Girl Next Door 19
In Answer to *How Are You?* 20
The Collector 21
Recovery 22
Timing 23
Second Hand Chance 24
We Used to Be Closer 25
I Put You on Speaker Phone 26
Mommy 28
Her Death 29
The Final Notice 30
Reunion 31
Crying During Acupuncture 32
Secrets 33
When Packing a Suitcase for the Afterlife Goes Wrong 34
Behold 35
Daily Chain 36

Ghost Poem

I went looking for my poet's voice in my childhood home
and found it in the floral wallpaper of my bedroom
I found it on the stairs to the second floor
where I had a memory of a past life in a castle

My dad is still standing on the stairs between the floors
He's got a book in his left hand and looks confused
Sometimes he steps down to sit in his easy chair
He looks for the TV remote that hasn't been invented yet

I looked for my voice in the back of my sister's closet
and found it among the dresses I wished were mine
among the mismatched winter mittens in the downstairs closet
and on every knick knack that I had to dust for my mother

I even found it on the cold linoleum floors
and under the fake brick living room paneling
It lives still in the rocks of the seascape framed picture
that hangs in a different house now

I'd like to stay on the phone with my boyfriend
while my brother Jim poses in his army uniform
but I'm distracted by the turntable
playing something by the Beatles
and I have a new poem to work on now

Black Bear

A week after burying my father
a large black bear was unleashed
for the purpose of chasing me
in the dirt-floored cellar
of my childhood home

A girl would have fit
through the one small window
in the corner of the dark room

But it took a woman
to break out the glass
and to dream the fear loose

The bear got in
It always does
The girl's safe haven
is the woman's trap

And there's only way
that the girl and the bear
can both be saved
The dreamer must wake up

Teacher's Pet

I don't take a pill for depression
because I don't want to lose the lesson
I'm the girl in the front row with my hand raised
because there is no wrong question

I don't bring an apple
or a knife to cut or butter up
I've given up my preoccupation with boys
Now I think about which black dress I'll wear to the funeral
and how to follow dry tears to their source

I know birds don't sing for my entertainment
and that every cast shadow hints the presence of soul
Today I learned that sparrows don't care who is looking
and that pretty birds hide from view

Flying Dreams

One day the brown chameleon wakes up blue
but I can only change my clothing
shop for every color of the rainbow
and stuff my closet full

Someone is always left out
in the game of musical chairs
and we're all as exposed as the naked emperor
who thought he was dressed in the fine clothes

One day the cocooned pupae wakes with wings
and an urge to fly 11,000 feet high
I wake up with a head full of unexamined dreams
like a kaleidoscope of monarchs hanging from a tree

When we were kids we believed
we were angels in training
and the wing bones on our backs were proof
We propelled ourselves in dreams about flying
but let no leg hang over the bed

Now we have insurance to scare off those bogeymen
and paper money promises that can't buy time
The monarchs are pretty but so short lived
and we don't have those flying dreams anymore

Monsters under the Bed

When the second shoe drops
where the dirt was swept under
in the childhood home
that burned to the ground
will it make a sound?

Will you hold your hands up to your ears
or hold your breath till someone listens?

If the shoe doesn't fit
how long will you wear it
before you ask

Whose shoe is it?
How many are there?
When was the first one lost?

I Don't See Blue

I mourn the loss of turquoise
and the richness of royal
Periwinkle, powder
Cobalt and cornflower

Sometimes black looks navy
Sometimes in the morning
I catch a glimpse of aquamarine
but by afternoon it all goes white

I imagine that gray is baby blue
and dream about the passion of indigo
I write about a robin's egg cracking
and the glass marble sparkle I knew in your eyes

But where is my bluebird of happiness,
my wonderful world of blue sky?
I imagine them off living a new life
with those who take them for granted

I strain to remember the Caribbean sea
The iridescence of clam shells in New England
The blue quilted jumper my mother dressed me in
while my sister wore red for school picture day

I Look Up
—For Kathy, January 29, 1948 – November 12, 2015

I look for her
on the tops of trees
I think she'd notice
that the poplar pods are empty

That they're shaped
like baby tulips
cups for the mysterious
drinks that keep me small
and made her so big

My eyes search the unseen
and when I lose what I need
I know she knows
there are holes like portals
where things fall through

There are places of comfort
at the tops of trees
where the tulips turn like bells
but never ring

where the lost and found mingle
but don't tell their secrets
where the ornaments of childhood
hang out of reach

How to Make a Freckle

There's a danger in looking too long
so I close my eyes

I let the sun start a fire on my lids
turn from magenta to bright red

I visualize it making a freckle
or dropping a spark of inspiration

If I sit long enough in its glow
it might illuminate a truth I am blind to

It might melt a cold grudge
or fuse meaning where there was none

My pupils track its source
a dream I store for the future

Holding my face up to its brilliance
I don't worship but I pray

Waiting to Be Saved

On a lazy Sunday
made for folksingers
for beatniks and people
that read Carl Sagan

I'm fishing for lines
in Pandora's box
A pink smart phone
set on Cupid's station

I'm looking for wells
to throw pennies into
or take them out

I'm waiting for the part
where the harmonica breaks in
and Leonard Cohen meets Suzanne

The part where Yoko Ono
tapes the sound of snow falling
and Richard Brautigan
writes my favorite poem

The one about waking
the fly on his napkin
so he can clean his classes
and watch a pretty girl

I'm waiting for words to sink in
and for the silence between them
For the blues guitar solo
that pierces like an arrow
and makes me stand up
for everything true

I'm Drawing on the Blank Slate of This Day

It all starts with a flower
doodled in winter
in black and white
and grows into a big bang
of colored scribbles and spirals
an immaculate conception
born from the underworld

It all depends on indirect attention
and knowing what to leave out
Each mark is a dream
that tells more than one truth
and believes in the existence
of the next page

Never Too Late

It's too late for Woodstock
but not for that leopard-skin pillbox-hat
the one Bob Dylan made fun of
and Jackie O passed over for pink

It's too late for a star on Hollywood Boulevard
to walk the red carpet
or become a Jungian psychologist

It's probably too late to hike the Camino
but not to see the cherry blossoms
in Washington D.C.

It's too late to wear a polka dot bikini
to live at the beach off writer's royalties
But it's never too late to know a groove from a rut
to wear your heart on your sleeve and let it break

It's never too late to put flowers on the table
to let the song birds of your childhood
sing like Jericho through middle age

To let them be blue
and enjoy them when their golden
to visit Claude Monet's garden in spring

Going Home

The last of the packing comes down to one question
Should I bring extra shoes or make room for a book
Guide to a Happy Life?

I'm still looking for a good Sinatra record
because he was to your generation
what the Beatles were to mine
and music is a memory that doesn't skip

I've made a list of dinners I want to cook
I'd like to read aloud to you
or talk about how it felt for you to have a father
who favored his son over his daughter
and what was it like to be separated
from your mother at such a young age

But it might make you uncomfortable to talk about that
like the time your voice shook when you spoke of menstruation
when you handed me a pamphlet with diagrams and drawings
of the female reproductive system

I think you'd rather tell me that you don't like Dr. Phil
but you love the host of America's Funniest Videos
You complain that the heat is going to kill you
you want the TV on but don't care what channel

Our days of taking trips together are over
We won't go to Provincetown, Martha's Vineyard or Nova Scotia
But I'll push you in your wheelchair to the physical therapist
in the shopping plaza where Bobby was hit by a car that broke his leg

I want to ask you what it's like to be waited on
after waiting on your father, your husband and nine kids
and what you think about when you're alone in the middle of the night
Will we all end up in dining rooms turned into bedrooms
in hospital beds that our grandkids want to wind up and down?

Ever since Jim and Dan died a month apart
I think I have to pack something black when I travel
Maybe we can visit their grave and get a tuna melt sandwich at the pier
or listen to the radio and watch the boats go by
like daddy did when he was alive

At home, I'll be patient when you panic at the top of the stairs
and berate yourself for not being able to walk without help
I'll be gentle when I wash your hair
I won't mention how hard you rubbed my scalp
with cheap shampoo that stung my eyes when I was a girl

I'll walk the beach at sunset and bring you a feather or a shell
I'll water your plants, even the perennials
and the trees that I don't think need watering
but you are sure they do

The Suitcase

The days are small
packed tightly together
Not much room
for last minute changes

I don't like cruises
have never been on one
I don't like to gamble
or get my hopes up
about an afterlife or God

I fear the waiting room
where people cough and no one talks
and there is no proof of heaven

I don't check my bags
because the subatomic particles
that look like me
are afraid of losing
and disappearing

Poetry is a passport
in the universal mother tongue
It's only 4% visible
and 96% dark riddle

I can write poetry
but can't take it with me
because science has proven
my suitcase is an illusion
filled with mostly empty space

Morning Commute

I woke up wanting to see
the crane migration in Nebraska
or at least an ostrich in the zoo

Clouds swept past my window
like a clock unwinding
like the ghosts of lost loved-ones departing

I woke up imagining
that I knew the names of birds
posed in the treetops
waiting to be photographed

The wind was like a speeding train
trying to squeeze its way inside
Leafless trees cowered
and mourned being left behind

I woke up worrying about lovers
abandoned by the loves of their lives
and blonde-haired children in Spiderman suits
who don't understand

I imagined people on planes
on their way to Australia
I tried but couldn't see their faces
buried in magazines

Yours is covered in blankets
that hide you from the sun
while your breath stitches a dream
about a quest of life or death

It's the dream that you'll tell during breakfast
when the steam of tea rises like smoke
and kitchen dishes clink like wheels on a track
on their way to a new unknown

Dream Inventory

The dream of the animal stuck on my head
The dream of the woman giving me the finger
The dream in which I yell to her "that's a load of crap"
and the one where I call your name out loud
and it wakes us both up

The dream about dog trainings on how not to kill chickens
The dream about my sister giving me a dress that doesn't fit
The dream where I walk to Roanoke wearing a kerchief in the rain
and the one where my mother says that I'm trying to claim her

All the dreams about children left in my care
and the disabled baby in the crib
All the dreams of being lost in unfamiliar places
and the cell phone with numbers that float like bubbles

The dream where the woman with black hair and long fingernails
lies when she says good things only happen to good people
The dream where I ask a different woman for directions
I believe her when she says "there are no turns"
"It's all the same long winding road"

Where I'm From

I am from a granite boulder seawall
and cotton candy at Paragon Park
I'm from blackberry stains and beach rose petals
catalpa beans and bamboo

I am from my father's eyes
after he saw the holocaust at Buchenwald
and the nape of my mother's neck
where white pearls hung
before her thyroid surgery

I am from Hail Mary full of grapes
midnight mass and pennies in the poor box
I'm from the unlucky luck of the Irish
the Old Sod and Southie
before there were gangsters

I am from A your Adorable
B you're so Beautiful
God Bless Mommy and Daddy
Jimmy and Kathy
Colleen and Danny
Sherry and Johnny
Joey and Bobby and Trish

I am from the salt of the earth
One if by land, two if by sea
John F. Kennedy and Fenway Park
even when the Red Sox are losing

I'm from ice skates and alphabet streets
jump ropes and black and white TV
I'm not from the farm or the city
I'm from plastic flowers in the village cemetery
and horseshoe crabs with blue blood

I'm from my grandmother's picnic basket
sleeping on curlers in baby doll pajamas
kerchiefs and bobby socks
hoola hoops and the twist
Dear Diary today is Friday

I'm from bad words crossed out
and secret codes not revealed

from Johnny on the Spot
hide-and-seek in the dark

I'm from hurricanes and floods
and Coast Guard rescue missions
from playing monopoly
with hidden stashes of money
by a kerosene lamp in the kitchen

Jim and Dan
James Michael Redman November 22, 1946 – July 25, 2001
Daniel Mark Redman October 7, 1951 – August 29, 2001

My brothers live in photo albums
They wear Red Sox shirts
and eat watermelon in summer

They go to casinos
and hit the jackpot
sing karaoke
and drink beer when they want to

From exotic places by the ocean
they watch girls in bikinis on the beach
or go out to concerts and baseball games
and watch the weather channel on TV

My brothers live like postcards now
I write, "I wish you were still here"
on the back of each one

No stamps
No addresses
Their eyes don't blink

They wave perpetually
from the places they have been
or put their paper thin arms
around me

They still have opinions
and loud Boston accents
It must be hard for them
to be so quiet

to live like rumors
and in snippets of dreams
that those who love them
write down and save

They live on paper now
like money that can't be spent
And I am like a teenager with a pop star crush
who kisses their 8 x 10s

My brothers would laugh out loud
at how odd it is to be dead
staring endlessly out from their glossy prints
while I am staring in

The Girl Next Door

I'm the woman who walks to the mailbox every day
whose life you imagine when you drive by and wave
The one collecting sticks for kindling as she walks
who stops reciting poetry out loud when she sees you
The homebody in house clothes with dirt smudged at the hips
seen swinging her arms up over her head
because studies have shown that symphony conductors
live longer than the rest of us

In Answer to *How Are You?*

I'm starting to like sauerkraut

I'm worried that the water
in the chicken coop has frozen

I need a haircut

And ever since I saw that serrated spoon
in the silverware drawer this morning
I've been thinking about grapefruit

Awesome is for narcissists
and fine is for china

Today I ordered a hat pin from Amazon
and googled "psychopaths that don't murder"

Good is for those absolved of sin
and well is for water

I keep a Scrabble dictionary
in the backseat of my car
and a kaleidoscope in my glove compartment

What else do you need to know?

The Collector

Leave me alone
to press my thoughts
rare flowers
in an hardcover book

Give me time to write lyrics
to the melody of morning
to pray on a rosary of silence

I need to measure each day
by the stretch of light and shadow
see the moon as a bowl
fired by the sun

I want to make a fossil
impressed with this feeling
until its innate memory shines

Let me steal a few moments
to collect an intuition
to look an untold story in the eye

Recovery

I wake cold turkey like clockwork
to the sound of your car driving away
Solitude is the fix I want to be alone with
but my tolerance for abandonment is low

I try not to think
about the clutter in the basement
or the rain washing foundations away
I recreate my life like a puzzle
Is everyone safe in their place?

I count the hours I've slept
like an addict counts pills
and then loses track

Sometimes I fall back to sleep
and imagine I'll never wake up
or I stare out the window
at the tree losing leaves
and wait for an urge to take shape

The unexpected poem
like a dream just recalled
is an escape route
that gets my attention

It's the transcendent intervention
of welcomed inspiration
the secret life I depend on
and the recovery I faithfully follow

Timing

I try to time the toasting
of the morning's sprouted bagel
so that the butter doesn't melt
before the eggs are boiled

The tea should still be hot
before the eggs have cooled down
before their gold is spread like wealth
on the new day's wheel of fortune

A pen should be nearby
and notebook pages spacious
The chair should be placed near a window
and in the best case scenario should rock

The disposition should be even
Not overly sunny or sullen
Silence should be noticed
Although words can be read out loud

Words can be tested for rhythm
Come together for unexpected meaning
They can be chosen for their freshness
and measured for preciseness

I try not to drip the yoke
that hardens like wax
down the front of my robe
or worry that inspiration
is like a meal too quickly consumed

The tea lingers the longest
It can be carried around
like a half-finished poem
sipped to the last cold drop
or forgotten

like the breakfast plate
haphazard in the sink
and the leftover crumbs
that have washed and settled
in trails that can never be followed

Second Hand Chance

I've written this poem before
It's like a movie I saw when I was young
that I can't remember the end to

There's a worn pathway that's easy to find
but there's also amnesia
and I can't take my eyes off
the point of remembering
as it is happening again

I flip TV channels
while the monarch butterflies
fly 3,000 miles fighting weather
and songbirds raise their pitch
to be heard above the human chatter

Second movies are like second teeth
We call second-round children grand
because they bring a second wind
to the lucid dream of life

Some of us will have second childhoods
Our car keys will be taken away
We'll eat too much sugar
and walk around in one slipper

I've written this poem before
I've written this poem before
But I can't remember the end

We Used to Be Closer

The moon is slipping away
Every year an inch further
Giving the earth the cold shoulder
Making each day a little longer

Every year the earth grows heavier
with the weight of space debris
with the loss of gravitational pull
and the moon's close affection

Like star crossed lovers
who've been taken for granted
who've lost their spark
over the past few billion years

The moon and the earth
are like an old married couple
facing the inevitable
and drifting apart

I Put You on Speaker Phone

Your room is yellow
quiet with a window
no roommates
no peanut butter crackers
for breakfast

You love the nurses
but want to go home
You thought your granddaughter
gave you a sponge bath

I laughed when I asked you
how many fingers I was holding up
but was really thinking
*How many daughters do you have
and do you know which one I am?*

When I was an infant in the hospital
I was separated from you for a month
And now it's me asking you
What do you need?

You said, "Bye honey
I love you" three times
but couldn't manage
to hang up the phone

"It's okay
Just pretend I'm sitting
in the chair by the window
You can forget I'm here
and take a nap"

"I wonder if it's still snowing"
you said after a long pause
and then "Now you sound gone"
"Are you still there, Coll?"

Holding the phone like a baby monitor
I heard you cough
and your amplified beating heart
as the omnipresent sound
a baby's life revolves around

What kind of voodoo is this?
I wondered if I was intruding
and briefly felt intruded upon
remembering being the child
who tried not to bother you

Maybe its time to navigate
those faraway connections
those unseen and blurred lines
where the dead and living mingle

That's the story I told myself
as I fixed my lunch and watched
the conspicuous phone
on the living room chair
until the connection timed out

Mommy

It's my mother in me
that couldn't cry
when I first heard she died
and my father in me
that broke down
when I saw her

It looked like she had one eye slightly open
as if asserting her motherly omnipresence
In life she didn't miss a trick
and never liked to feel left out

She left this world on August 15th
the day Catholics celebrate the Ascension
of Mother Mary into heaven
We were just glad it didn't happen the day before
on our brother Bobby's birthday

Our sister Sherry shopped for the dress
that she wore in the casket
and splurged on earrings
she knew she'd like

It was like shopping for
the birthday or Christmas gifts
she stopped wanting to get
and that we could never give her again

My mother stopped collecting stuff
long before she forgot dates
and caring about the outside world
But she never forgot her nine children's names
and the three who had passed before her

Always hard working
and always beautiful
Now she looked peaceful
but a faint frown hung on

As if to show a hint of resistance
or a fading expression of her recent refrain
"I don't like this place
and I want to go home"

It was the child in me
that could only call her "mommy"
when I gazed into her face for the last time
and imagined where her home would be now

Her Death

The knife went in
but didn't come out
I tracked the pain
and point of entry
while half asleep
and half awake

While you were dreaming
of her body in the casket
and draining her blood
behind the funeral parlor
because no one else would do it

No one twisted it
No one cried
No one was stabbed in the back

Now the memory barely exists
but it exacts a secret cost
like a baby's wail
between the in and out breath
hangs silent in the air

It's carried and passed on
sealed like a letter
just one in a stack
of Dear John complaints
that no one has the heart to read

The Final Notice
- For Danny

Now that your ghost is 65
they want to sell you life insurance

Now that you've been dead for 15 years
the AARP wants to claim you

The VA wants a donation
for the return address labels
from places you don't live

Social Security recommends a supplement plan
but only during Open Enrollment

It's time for a colonoscopy
now that your ghost is having a birthday

Everyone has a plan
that you can't live without

The junk mail keeps coming
but you don't

It warns: Please open immediately
No postage is necessary
This is your final notice

Reunion

I wanted to see you
and not look away
but you looked away first

You wrapped yourself
in a royal blue blanket
and laid on the floor
next to our mother

I wanted her to turn
and comfort you
but she was wrapped up too

You made your choice
with no words spoken
laying down your life
before it was taken

Becoming one of two
in solemn reunion
like bound cocoons
wait for transformation

Crying During Acupuncture

Pricked at birth
The sting still hurts

Now my stiffened knee
is loosening

Now one tear falls
for two losses

A mirror speck
that holds the past

The tear my mother
couldn't shed

The one my sister
couldn't hold back

It swelled then slipped
like a clean drop of rain

Like a gem of truth
snapped from a necklace

Down my cheek
in undistorted release

A precious pearl
hard earned

Secrets

Some stories are like secrets
that we gave up for adoption
We want to claim our children
but have forfeited the right

So we wait to be asked
by those who want to know
We hope for reunion
and to feel complete

Some stories are like the iris
that I discovered as a girl
growing by an abandoned house
that we all thought was haunted

Exotic like an orchid
that didn't belong
I only ever picked dandelions
for my mother

Some stories are like card games
and you're holding someone's ace
You want to give it back
but not be seen

You want to even the score
but not at the expense of another
You want the royal flush
and not the bluff
of being loved

When Packing a Suitcase for the Afterlife Goes Wrong

You dream about a layover
and drinking tea at a café
that's like your teenage hangout
but different

There's a stranger you want to impress
and your bags have all been lost
You're trying not to panic
because you forgot
to claim them

But then they come
opened and spilled
with everything strewn
in every direction

Not just clothes
but a yard sale of junk
and nothing fits
where it once did
and nothing feels like yours

You leave the mess
but vow to come back
You can't sort it out
and your bus is arriving

It takes the long loop
of a familiar route
Just you and the driver
You sit half-way back

You watch sunset turn to dusk
as if you never left
as if there was no difference
between leaving and coming home

Be Hold

Don't over water
Please climb
Take time in the dark

Some roots
collide with cement
and win the battle against it

Some insight comes
from closing a door
and looking out for others

Don't underestimate
The weight of a petal
What we see
and what we don't
are equal

Daisy Chain

At first glance
one looks like the other
But each is unique

And the pattern they make
is the allure of the story
and the body we cling to

Some are held dear
others hang by a thread

Still others are tightened by knots
that must be untangled in the end

Or chewed off
the way a serpent eats its own tail

It distances itself from its birth
and ends up where it starts

He loves me, he loves me not
is the question we weigh as we string them

She loves me, she loves me not
Will the chain of days be long enough?

The childhood ones are as faded
as the final ones will be

All are fragile for better or worse
and all are worthy of cherishing

www.ingramcontent.com/pod-product-compliance
Lightning Source LLC
LaVergne TN
LVHW041556070426
835507LV00011B/1121